Terrorist
Dossiers

TARGETING TERROR

Counterterrorist
RAIDS

Samuel M. KATZ

Lerner Publications Company/Minneapolis

Publishers Note: The information in this book was current at the time of publication. However, the publisher is aware that news involving current events dates quickly. Please refer to the websites on page 69 for places to go to obtain up-to-date information.

Lerner Publications Company
A division of Lerner Publishing Group
241 First Avenue North
Minneapolis, MN 55401

Website address: www.lernerbooks.com

Library of Congress Cataloging-in-Publication Data

Katz, Samuel M., 1963–
      Targeting terror : counterterrorist raids / by Samuel M. Katz.
         p. cm. — (Terrorist dossiers)
      Includes bibliographical references and index.
      ISBN: 0–8225–1568–7 (lib. bdg. : alk. paper)
      1. Terrorism—Prevention—Case studies. 2. Special operations (Military science)—Case studies. I. Title.
      HV6431.K319 2005
      363.32—dc22   2004006498

Manufactured in the United States of America
1 2 3 4 5 6 – DP – 10 09 08 07 06 05

CONTENTS

WHO'S WHO AND
WHAT'S WHAT

Afganistan: a country in central Asia. The Taliban, an Islamic fundamentalist group, seized power in Afghanistan in 1992. The Taliban was accused of harboring al-Qaeda terrorists after the September 11, 2001, attacks in the United States. In late 2001, the United States and Great Britain joined with internal Afghan forces and overthrew the Taliban.

cell: a small unit of an organization or movement

Osama bin Laden: the founder and commander of al-Qaeda

al-Qaeda: an Islamic fundamentalist terrorist group founded in about 1989 and commanded by Osama bin Laden. Al-Qaeda's goal is a global jihad (holy war) uniting Islamic movements around the world.

reconnaissance: an exploration of enemy territory

September 11, 2001: the date of a major terrorist attack against the United States. On this date, al-Qaeda terrorists crashed airplanes into targets in the United States, killing approximately three thousand people.

sniper: a sharpshooter who specializes in shooting individuals from a hidden position

Taliban: a strict Islamic fundamentalist government that held power in Afghanistan from 1996 to 2001 and supported and protected Osama bin Laden and al-Qaeda

terrorism: violent acts used to frighten civilians or to pressure governments into making changes

22 Special Air Service (SAS): An elite British counterterrorist force

INTRODUCTION

The satellite images and aerial reconnaissance photos were crystal clear. Using state-of-the-art equipment, the operators had pinpointed the radio and cellular phone messages to an area in southeastern Afghanistan, near the Pakistan border.

The team from Britain's famed 22 Special Air Service (SAS) regiment spent most of the day preparing for the night's operation—a search-and-destroy raid. Heavily armed and carrying loads of equipment on their backs, the SAS squadrons would cover large stretches of terrain and raid al-Qaeda and Taliban bases in the mountain caves.

The commander briefed the men for nearly an hour. He gave them the latest information about the enemy, passwords, evacuation and escape plans, radio frequencies, and rules of fighting. Darkness had engulfed the camp. It was time to go.

A small fleet of Chinook helicopters carried the operators toward the landing zone. That was the easy part. Most of the terrain would be covered on foot. The march across slippery slopes and deep ravines would take until dawn. Landmines and booby traps were scattered around the mountain pass. Al-Qaeda snipers were known to be active in the area.

The terrorists had placed several lookouts outside the caves that April night. The sentries knew the Afghan darkness. They knew the direction of the winds and the sounds of night. Yet they never heard the bullets being readied inside the SAS rifles. Nor could they sense that their heads were being tracked precisely through the crosshairs of high-powered rifle sights.

The operators, moving swiftly and methodically, entered the connecting complex of caves, shooting at anyone and everyone they encountered. By dawn, when the Chinooks emerged over the snowcapped peaks to pick up the SAS operators, eighteen terrorists lay dead. The operators had seized laptop computers, satellite cell phones, and stacks of documents for analysis. Perhaps, intelligence gathered from this raid would play a role—if only a small one—in the capture or killing of al-Qaeda leader Osama bin Laden himself.

The global war on terrorism began on September 11, 2001, when al-Qaeda terrorists crashed three airplanes into targets in the United States (a fourth crash-landed in a field in Pennsylvania), killing approximately three thousand people. Afterward, governments around the world set out to fight such groups as al-Qaeda.

The war on terrorism has been called the Fourth World War. The First and Second World Wars of the twentieth century were conventional military campaigns. During these wars, soldiers fought visible enemies on battlefields that could be marked off on maps. The Third World War was the Cold War—fought between the United States and the former Soviet Union. This "war" was actually a clash of ideas—specifically, the Soviet philosophy of communism versus the U.S. ideals of democracy.

This newest world war is a far more frightening conflict. Terrorist fighters are not part of large armies. They work in small groups, or cells, that can be hard to find. They operate from secret bases spread around the world. They often kill civilians—people who are not members of the military—and use religious beliefs to justify their violent acts. Terrorism shows no signs of slowing.

Counterterrorists are government operatives who are trained to fight terrorism. To do their work, counterterrorist operators must think and operate like the terrorists they combat.

Although the new war on terrorism began on September 11, 2001, terrorism and counterterrorism are much older. Since the mid-twentieth century, counterterrorists have been hitting terrorists where they live, where they work, and where they hide. Operations have ranged from gunning down a single terrorist chieftain to carrying out major battalion-sized assaults. This book will examine some of the boldest, most important, and most awe-inspiring counterterrorist operations in modern history.

WHO'S WHO AND
WHAT'S WHAT

Arabs: a group of people who speak Arabic and share a common history and culture. Most Arabs live in the Middle East, but many have emigrated to Asia, North Africa, Europe, and the United States.

Black September: a Palestinian terrorist group founded in 1971

casualty: injury or death in context of battle or war

commandos: soldiers trained to take part in hit-and-run or raiding operations behind enemy lines

Democratic Front for the Liberation of Palestine (DFLP): a Palestinian terrorist group founded in 1969

Flotilla 13: an elite unit of Israeli naval commandos

Israel: a Middle Eastern country formed in 1948 as a Jewish homeland. Citizens of Israel are known as Israelis, and the country's official language is Hebrew.

Lebanon: a Middle Eastern country north of Israel. Lebanon has served as a base of operations for many Palestinian terrorist groups.

Middle East: a geographical and political term referring to nations in eastern North Africa and southwestern Asia

Munich Olympics: the 1972 Summer Olympic Games in Munich, West Germany, at which Palestinian terrorists kidnapped and killed eleven members of the Israeli Olympic team

Palestinian Liberation Organization (PLO): an umbrella
group founded in 1964 to represent all Palestinian
movements. The PLO's chief goal is to establish a state
for Palestinians in territory currently controlled by
Israel. The PLO is regarded by some as legitimate and by
others as a terrorist organization.

Palestinians: an ethnic group native to the ancient
region of Palestine. In modern times, Palestine consists
of Israel and the occupied territories (areas adjacent
to and controlled by Israel since 1967). Many
Palestinians no longer live in this region but instead
make their homes in other parts of the world.

paratroopers: soldiers trained to parachute out of
airplanes

Sayeret Mat'kal: an elite Israeli counterterrorist unit

Yasser Arafat: a leader within the Palestinian Liberation
Organization and figurehead of the Palestinian cause

THE MOTHER OF ALL OPERATIONS: OPERATION SPRING OF YOUTH

Sitting in their rented car, the operators nervously clutched their submachine guns outside the block of luxury apartments on Rue Verdun in fashionable West Beirut, Lebanon. Other operators clutched sleek AK-47 Kalashnikov assault rifles. As an armored Lebanese police car rolled slowly down the boulevard, four men—dressed as hippies with long hair and T-shirts—emerged from the vehicle with suitcases in hand.

Two other rented cars emerged from the shadows and pulled up behind the first, their engines still running. The passengers emerged from the vehicles quickly. Some also looked like hippies. Others looked like attractive blondes, with stunning figures and heavy blue handbags.

Beirut, Lebanon, is the capital of Lebanon. The city served as a safe haven for several Black September leaders in the early 1970s.

The hippies and "women" crossed the street. They approached two black Mercedes staffed by three Palestine Liberation Organization (PLO) bodyguards. The three were instantly cut down with bursts of rifle fire.

As the spent rifle shells rolled into the gutter, along with the blood of the killed sentries, the operators entered the building. The operation was under way.

■ ■

TERROR AND COUNTERTERROR

The operation in Beirut was payback for a massacre at the 1972 Munich Olympics. During the games, Palestinian terrorists, demanding the release of two hundred Arab prisoners in Israel, had killed eleven Israeli athletes. The massacre, broadcast live on television, shocked and horrified the international community. It created fear throughout the world and sparked barely containable anger inside Israel. Israel vowed revenge.

A Black September terrorist peers from the window of an apartment at the Munich Summer Olympics. Israeli athletes are held hostage inside.

Immediately after the attack, Israeli prime minister Golda Meir ordered her intelligence service and military commanders to develop a plan to wipe out Black September—the Palestinian faction that had carried out the attack.

From November 1972 to the spring of 1973, Israeli agents traveled through the streets and back alleys of Europe and the Middle East, selectively hunting down men on Israel's Black September most wanted list. Black September was on the run and in disarray, but it was far from defeated. If Israel wanted to truly stop Black September, it would have to strike the group at its Beirut headquarters. The mission, scheduled for April 9, 1973, became known as Operation Spring of Youth.

THE STRIKE

The Israelis planned five separate operations, each with its own code name. Target Aviva would be carried out by Sayeret Mat'kal, Israel's top counterterrorist unit. On this mission, operators would assassinate three top Black September commanders, who all lived in the same luxury high-rise on Rue Verdun in West Beirut. Target Gilah consisted of a paratrooper raid on the headquarters of the Democratic Front for the Liberation of Palestine (DFLP), another PLO faction. Target Tzilah involved the destruction of a major PLO arms depot near the outskirts of Beirut. Target Vardah had naval commandos from Israel's famed Flotilla 13 blowing up an explosives lab near the Lebanese coast. Target Yehudit was a strike against a Black September base north of the Lebanese city of Sidon.

Ehud Barak, shown here in combat gear, dressed as a woman for Operation Spring of Youth

The Target Aviva operation was led by Lieutenant Colonel Ehud Barak. His team would work in plainclothes, most of them dressed as hippies. To maximize the masquerade, some of the commandos would dress as women. Lieutenant Colonel Barak would don a blonde wig and add mountains of tissue inside a borrowed bra to create a feminine figure.

OPERATION GIFT:
THE UNLUCKY THIRTEEN IN BEIRUT

Operation Spring of Youth was not the first visit by Sayeret Mat'kal to the shores of Beirut. On December 28, 1968, Sayeret Mat'kal struck Beirut International Airport in a raid designed for symbolism as well as destruction.

In the months before the raid, Palestinian terrorists had used the airport as a base of operations. From there they had traveled to Europe and then hijacked Israeli, U.S., and European aircraft. Security guards in Lebanon had turned a blind eye to Palestinian men boarding aircraft with weapons and grenades in their carry-on bags.

On November 26, 1968, at the Athens airport in Greece, two Palestinian terrorists fired automatic weapons at an El Al (Israel's national airline) airplane on the ground. An Israeli passenger was killed, and an Israeli flight attendant was wounded. The aircraft suffered serious damage. Israel vowed revenge.

The mission, dubbed Operation Gift, was to destroy as many Arab owned airplanes as possible and to damage important airport facilities, such as fuel silos. Civilian casualties were to be avoided at all costs.

The commando task force would be transported to the Lebanese capital on helicopters. Naval boats and naval commandos would be waiting offshore, in case the task force needed to be rescued. The assault force was divided into three groups, each targeting a different part of the airport. The commandos were told to destroy Arab-owned aircraft with explosives—but only after it was determined, beyond a reasonable doubt, that there was no one on board.

The helicopters lifted off from Israel shortly after 9:00 P.M. on December 28. The operators dropped nails along the roadway leading to the airport to damage the tires of any police units responding to the attack. They dropped smoke and lit flares to add to the overall confusion. The chaos was absolute. The traffic jam was so horrific that even fire and police cars were stuck in the gridlock.

The commandos had little difficulty carrying out their mission. Security forces ran for their lives at the sight of the Israeli operators, who fired their Uzi submachine guns into the darkened December sky as a warning. In all, the commandos destroyed thirteen aircraft belonging to Middle East Airlines, Libyan International Airways, and Trans Mediterranean Airlines, all Arab-owned companies. The entire raid lasted only twenty-five minutes. The Israeli choppers lifted off from a runway lit up by burning airplanes. No civilians were harmed in the operation. ∎

■ ■

Target Aviva began at 2:00 A.M. on April 9. *The hit teams left their vehicles nonchalantly, tossing their cigarettes onto the curb before grabbing their weapons and racing into action. Inside the first building, the operators removed their wigs and sprinted up the brightly lit stairway to the sixth floor. Their first stop was the door of Abu Yusef, the Black September mastermind who had planned the Munich Olympic Massacre. The Israeli team leader, Major Yoni Netanyahu, took plastic explosives from a brown leather suitcase and quickly blew the front door off its hinges. Four Israelis burst through the apartment and found Abu Yusef desperately searching for the assault rifle that PLO leader Yasser Arafat had given him. Yusef was killed by a thirty-round burst of fire from Netanyahu's submachine gun.*

Yasser Arafat, the longtime leader of the PLO

At the same time, two other teams entered an adjacent building on Rue Verdun and visited the apartments of two more Black September masterminds, Kamal A'dwan and Kamal Nasser. Both men were dead in a matter of minutes. By the time the operators made it downstairs, they found their comrades engaged in a desperate close-quarters gunfight with a few dozen Lebanese security officers. Determined not to let anything get between them and the evacuation back to Israel, the Israeli commandos beat off the responding Lebanese troops and guerilla fighters.

Israeli drivers performed some race carlike stunts and headed for the Mediterranean Sea at top speed. There, the commandos and drivers abandoned the rented vehicles, grabbed suitcases full of documents taken from the targeted apartments, and headed back to sea on rubber dinghies.

Across town, outside the headquarters of the DFLP, a fierce gun battle had developed between a dozen paratroopers and nearly one hundred terrorists. The paratroopers, also dressed as hippies, fired at the DFLP terrorists at close range. The Palestinian defense was determined. But DFLP gunmen on the building's upper floors took the elevator to the battle on the street, not realizing that Israeli commandos were waiting with their guns aimed at the elevator door. The moment the elevator reached the ground floor and the doors opened, the Israelis opened up with everything they had. Once the shooting stopped, the commandos raced to the elevator, removed the dead bodies, and sent the car back to the top floor. This process was repeated several times before the DFLP gunmen on the upper floors realized what was happening.

Members of the Democratic Front for the Liberation of Palestine, a major PLO faction, meet in Beirut.

Unlike Target Aviva, the raid on DFLP headquarters cost the Israelis dearly. Two paratroopers were killed, and several more were seriously wounded. To save his remaining men, the unit commander called in the air force for an evacuation. Israeli Air Force helicopters descended on Beirut to rescue the commandos.

Operation Spring of Youth's three other missions were all handled perfectly and without an Israeli death or injury. All the targets were destroyed. For Black September, Operation Spring of Youth was a serious defeat. With its commanders assassinated, the organization became ineffective. Yet, in the years to come, the group was replaced by an even more violent and bolder generation of Palestinian terrorists.

WHO'S WHO AND WHAT'S WHAT

Islam: a religion founded on the Arabian Peninsula in the seventh century A.D. by the prophet Muhammad. The religion's primary tenets are known as the Five Pillars of Islam. Its holy book is the Quran.

Islamic fundamentalism: a school of thought that supports a return to traditional Islamic ideas and government and opposes Western (European and American) influence on the Islamic world. Most Islamic fundamentalists do not advocate terrorism.

Libya: a North African nation west of Egypt. Libyan leader Muammar Qadhafi has been linked to terrorist operations worldwide.

Muammar Qadhafi: the leader of Libya's government since 1969. Qadhafi has been accused of supporting terrorist groups around the world.

Pan Am 103: a U.S. airliner blown up over Scotland in 1988. The bombing was carried out by Palestinians, assisted by Libyan agents.

radar: a system for detecting objects by means of high-frequency radio waves. The waves bounce off of objects and then return to the radar station, allowing operators to pinpoint the objects' locations.

The United States Strikes Back:
Operation
El Dorado Canyon

The mood was tense inside the Pentagon's Command Center, headquarters of the U.S. military. For many years, the United States had chosen not to retaliate against attacks by terrorists. U.S. citizens had been victims, yet the government had not sought revenge. Nor had it struck out at terrorists to discourage them from future attacks.

Most of the terrorist attacks against U.S. citizens had occurred in the Middle East or North Africa. Some of the attackers were Palestinians, angered by U.S. support for Israel. Others were Islamic groups (Islam is the dominant religion in the Middle East) who disliked American values.

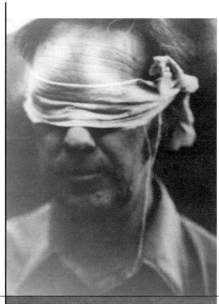

A blindfolded American embassy hostage held by Iranian extremists in 1979

The attacks started with the brutal assassination of a U.S. diplomat in Khartoum, Sudan, in 1973. The killing had been carried out by Palestinians, operating under orders from Yasser Arafat. Then Islamic extremists seized the U.S. Embassy in Tehran, Iran, in 1979, taking a group of Americans hostage. In 1983 Islamic terrorists bombed the U.S. Embassy in Beirut, Lebanon, killing 63 people. Later in the year, a suicide truck bomber struck a U.S. Marine Corps barracks in Beirut, killing 241 marines. The hostage taking, hijackings, and killings continued. Within twelve years, nearly 500 U.S. citizens—soldiers, diplomats, and civilians—were killed. Americans were angry. U.S. generals argued that the United States needed to retaliate.

Finally, the United States decided to act. It would strike out against a corrupt nation—Libya. Libya had supported terrorists in many countries, financed their operations, and dispatched terrorist squads to strike against U.S. interests worldwide. By hitting Libya, the United States wanted to send a message throughout the terrorist underground: "If you attack us, we will kill you!"

On April 15, 1986, U.S. generals monitored radar screens, maps, and communications devices. The call came out: "Aircraft approaching Libyan air space. . . ."

This was it. The United States was finally retaliating.

TERROR AND COUNTERTERROR
For years, Libya had threatened the United States. Shortly after Ronald Reagan was sworn in as U.S. president in 1981, reports hinted that "Libyan hit teams" had snuck into the United States to try to assassinate the president. Five years later, on March 24, 1986, Libya fired six surface-to-air missiles at U.S. Navy jets over the Gulf of Sidra near the Libyan coast. The navy eventually destroyed Libyan missile and radar bases as a warning to Libyan ruler Muammar Qadhafi that any fight with the United States would be a one-sided contest. But shortly after the incident, a Libyan missile boat threatened U.S. Navy warships, which then destroyed the boat.

Then, on April 5, 1986, a small yet powerful bomb ripped through the crowded dance floor at La Belle Discotheque in West Berlin, a popular hangout for U.S. soldiers stationed in Germany. The device had been concealed in a travel bag and left behind on the floor. It packed a lethal punch, killing a U.S. Army sergeant and a Turkish woman and seriously wounding 230 others, including 41 U.S. soldiers.

President Reagan decided to strike back. He ordered his top military commanders to draw up a plan to punish Libya for carrying out state-sponsored terrorist attacks against the United States. The mission was code named Operation El Dorado Canyon.

The United States was determined to make the operation as straightforward—yet as spectacular—as possible. Operation El Dorado Canyon would be an air strike designed to cripple Libya's terrorist system. The mission included five targets:

The bombing of La Belle Discotheque killed two adults and injured many more.

- The Aziziyah Barracks in Tripoli, capital of Libya and headquarters for Libyan terrorism
- Military facilities at Tripoli's international airport
- The Side Bilal naval base on Libya's Mediterranean coast, used to train terrorists in underwater sabotage
- The Jamahiriyah military barracks and terrorist facility
- The Benina air base southeast of Benghazi, Libya

All the targets were protected by an extensive air defense network consisting of radar systems, surface-to-air missiles, antiaircraft artillery, and jet fighters. U.S. generals thought it would be safest to attack all five targets at once. In all, nearly one hundred air force and navy combat aircraft would be needed to carry out the operation.

THE STRIKE

On the night of April 15, twenty-nine U.S. F-111 bombers took off from British bases under cover of darkness and a blanket of secrecy. Their mission involved the targets in and around Tripoli. A-6 Intruder attack jets would handle the targets in and around Benghazi. The aircraft would all strike at the same time. The air force and navy would also dispatch planes with jamming devices that would disable Libyan radio and radar systems.

The U.S. strike on Tripoli in 1986 destroyed residential areas as well as military targets.

The first one-thousand-pound bombs began to rain down on Tripoli and Benghazi at 1:58 A.M. on April 16. Thanks to the jamming devices, Libya never knew the Americans were coming. The Libyan air force never sent up a single plane to meet the U.S. bombers. The buildings selected for destruction were all hit with great accuracy. Unfortunately, some civilian buildings were hit too, especially in Tripoli, where the terrorists made their headquarters near residential areas. Dozens were killed, including one of Qadhafi's adopted daughters. Nearly one hundred people were wounded. All the U.S. aircraft but one returned to base safely. The exception was an F-111 hit by ground artillery fire. Both F-111 pilots were killed.

Operation El Dorado Canyon was the United States' first true statement that terrorism would no longer be tolerated. For two years afterward, Libya scaled back its terrorist activities. But Qadhafi's inactions would be short-lived. On December 21, 1988, Libyan agents assisted Palestinian terrorists in blowing up Pan Am 103, a U.S. airliner, in the skies over Lockerbie, Scotland. Two hundred and seventy people died in the bombing. For reasons never explained, the United States chose not to retaliate militarily for that act of mass murder.

Army Commando Regiment: a special operations force, created by the Sri Lankan government to fight the Liberation Tigers of Tamil Eelam

Liberation Tigers of Tamil Eelam (LTTE): the largest and most militant group fighting for a Tamil state within Sri Lanka

refugee: a person who flees to a foreign country to escape danger or persecution at home

Sinhalese: the largest ethnic group in Sri Lanka. The Sinhalese practice Buddhism and speak Sinhalese. They hold the most power in the Sri Lankan government.

Sri Lanka: an island nation in the Indian Ocean, located about twenty miles off the Indian coast

Tamils: the second largest ethnic group in Sri Lanka, making up about 18 percent of the population. They speak Tamil, and most of them practice the Hindu religion.

HUNTING THE HUNTERS:
OPERATION LIBERATION

The **Sri Lankan terrorists** felt they had thought of everything to safeguard their territory. Makeshift explosive mines were hidden in banana trees, attached to near-invisible trip wires. When activated, the mines would blast shrapnel (shell fragments) into anyone in a fifty-yard radius. Conventional landmines, too, were hidden inside the jungle brush. Booby traps, such as pits filled with spikes, were scattered along the roads.

But on this day in May 1987, the terrorists knew something was wrong because the jungle was too silent. Their squads watched and waited for what they thought would be a massive ground assault on

Members of the Liberation Tigers of Tamil Eelam, a fierce
Sri Lankan terror organization

their jungle strongholds. But they had misjudged the situation. Instead of a ground assault, the attack would come from the sea.

Sri Lankan army commandos, with black and green stripes of paint on their faces, emerged from rubber dinghies in the calm Indian Ocean surf to hit the terrorists from behind. Soon the night was engulfed by the zigzagging light show of tracer rounds (illuminated ammunition) launched from many different directions. The terrorists had been hit by an invisible force in the darkness.

TERROR AND COUNTERTERROR The terrorists were members of the Liberation Tigers of Tamil Eelam (LTTE), or Tamil Tigers. The Tamils are a minority ethnic group in Sri Lanka (an island country off the coast of India). They have felt oppressed by the majority Sinhalese, an ethnic group that has historically held the most power in the nation. The LTTE wanted Tamil people to have their own independent state within Sri Lanka. The Tigers used terrorist tactics to fight the Sri Lankan government.

The Tigers began terrorizing Sri Lanka in the late 1970s. They were known to be fanatical warriors. Their operators had been said to swallow deadly cyanide tablets rather than surrender to government agents. They were also masters of the crossfire (hitting targets from two sides) and the ambush. In the years of bloody conflict against the Sri Lankan military, the Tigers had proven adept at hit-and-run attacks. Operating in small squads, they would emerge from the jungle in formation to strike government troops.

The Sri Lankan military decided to fight back using a language the terrorists understood—the language of knives slitting throats. So the Sri Lankan military created a special force, the Army Commando Regiment, that would fight the Tamil terrorists like terrorists. The commandos would attack with no mercy and would not follow the traditional rules of warfare.

Trained by the British SAS, the Sri Lankan commandos learned how to intimidate the enemy with words. The commandos spread rumors that the red berets they wore were colored with the blood of terrorists seized in combat.

By 1987 Sri Lankan leaders faced a point of no return. In the Jaffna Peninsula of northern Sri Lanka, Tamil attacks against the military

Inset: President Jayawardene was determined to crush the Tamil Tigers.
Above: A Tamil refugee family in India

had been fierce. Soldiers were afraid to leave their barracks. They rarely ventured out except to take revenge against Tamil people who aided LTTE terrorists. The attacks and counterattacks created a severe refugee crisis. More than 200,000 Tamils fled to nearby India as a result of the fighting near their homes. In May 1987, Sri Lankan president J. R. Jayawardene decided to unleash the Army Commando Regiment against the LTTE in the Jaffna Peninsula. The campaign became known as Operation Liberation.

To make the terrorists think a conventional attack was coming, Sri Lankan troops began their attack with shelling from naval boats. On May 18, a column of troops marched northwest from Elephant Pass toward Jaffna. The terrorists thought this column was the main attack force. Two days later, government forces launched additional diversionary attacks—meant to distract the terrorists from the real assault. Then, on May 26, Operation Liberation began in full.

THE STRIKE

Under the cover of darkness, a 180-man force from the Commando Regiment attacked from the sea, landing on the *northeastern Jaffna coast in rubber dinghies. The commandos took the beach unopposed. They raced into the jungle to cut off the Tigers' traditional escape routes. Attacking in small formations, usually 12-man teams, the commandos turned Tiger territory into a maze of death and destruction. Forced to fight on the commandos' terms, the terrorists became disoriented and uncoordinated. The hunters became the hunted. Tiger squads, expert in ambush warfare, were themselves ambushed. Landmines, once the Tigers' most effective weapon, were used with lethal effectiveness against them.*

The seaborne commandos boxed the Tamil fighters into a zone from which they could not escape. Hundreds of terrorists were killed in the fighting—much of it at close range. The commandos, moving on foot, advanced faster than even they thought possible. They managed to hit many Tiger camps with the terrorists still asleep in their beds. They seized an enormous amount of weapons and intelligence—files, photos, and a list of operatives—that was crucial in helping the government break up numerous terrorist cells.

In attacking from the east and striking by surprise with such speed, firepower, and sheer resolve, the commandos managed to do exactly what their SAS instructors had taught them—create fear. Within days of the landing, the sight of the red berets on patrol and inside Tamil villages was enough to secure villagers' cooperation. Communities that had once sheltered terrorists were wary of even offering them food or harmless assistance.

Within a week, it was clear to military commanders in Colombo, the Sri Lankan capital, that the campaign had been a smashing success. The LTTE withdrew from the areas under government attack, and its control in the Jaffna Peninsula weakened. India, worried about the violence and flood of refugees, eventually sent a peacekeeping force to the troubled land. India's entry into the conflict sparked another round of LTTE violence and terrorism, causing India to withdraw its troops in 1990. The LTTE continued fighting for Tamil self-rule and added new tactics, such as suicide bombing, to its arsenal. The violence lasted throughout the 1990s.

WHO'S WHO AND WHAT'S WHAT

British government: operating from London, England, the authority that maintains political control in Northern Ireland

Northern Ireland: the northern portion of the island of Ireland. Northern Ireland is a political division of the United Kingdom, along with England, Scotland, and Wales. Ethnically, Northern Ireland's population is split between Protestants and Catholics. (About half the population of is Protestant, while most of the rest is Catholic.) Protestants in Northern Ireland tend to identify with the people and culture of Britain, while Catholics there tend to identify with the people and culture of the Republic of Ireland to the south.

Provisional Irish Republican Army (PIRA): Northern Ireland's largest terrorist group. The PIRA and other terrorist groups have struck out at British targets in Northern Ireland and Great Britain.

Royal Ulster Constabulary (RUC): Northern Ireland's police force, renamed the Police Service of Northern Ireland in 2001

surveillance: keeping a close watch on a person or organization

ACTION AND REACTION:
OPERATIONS
JUDY AND FLAVIUS

ever turn off the engine. *That was an unwritten rule.* *During ambush operations, British operators were forbidden to shut off their car engines while waiting for targets to approach them. They had to be able to shift their vehicles into gear and drive off without any risk of stalling. Hesitation—stalling—was a recipe for a bullet in the head in Northern Ireland. So when locals saw a battered car with its engine running outside a pub or a police station, they knew that something violent was about to happen. The residents of the six counties of Northern Ireland were expert at sensing British forces, especially the dreaded killers of 22 SAS.*

The men sitting at the intersection near Falls Road that rain-swept night in Belfast, Northern Ireland, were spread among three cars. Their hands caressed the cold steel of their weapons. The men wondered what it would be like when the PIRA vehicles came near. Would the operation go smoothly, as it had in training? Or would it be a bloody mess?

TERROR AND COUNTERTERROR
The PIRA, short for Provisional Irish Republican Army, wants Northern Ireland and Ireland to be united. It also wants the British government to give up its control of Northern Ireland. In 1986, after nearly six years of deadly bombing attacks inside England, the PIRA adopted a different tactic. It began striking out against British security forces in Northern Ireland, including Irish police officers, British soldiers, and British intelligence

agents. The bloody campaign was designed to make these security forces fear patrolling the streets.

The British forces, including intelligence, counterterrorism, and SAS operatives, began fighting these tactics with advanced monitoring of the most wanted Irish terrorists. The British secretly watched the terrorists' movements using videotape, bugged phone lines, and old-fashioned detective work. The effort was massive in size and scope. Much of Britain's intelligence system was assigned to Northern Ireland, yet it

British soldiers dressed in riot gear prepared to deal harshly with protesters in Northern Ireland.

failed, for the most part, to thwart PIRA attacks. In 1987 alone, Irish terrorists carried out twenty-two bombing and machine-gun assaults against offices of the Royal Ulster Constabulary (RUC—the Northern Ireland police, renamed the Police Service of Northern Ireland in 2001). Dozens of RUC officers were assassinated.

For protection against terror attacks, most RUC stations were built like fortresses. They were covered by steel fencing, designed to defeat devices such as barrel-bombs (huge bombs hurled from trucks) and rocket-propelled grenades. Yet the PIRA always thought of ways to outsmart the RUC. For instance, to attack well-fortified RUC police stations, the Irish rammed them with construction equipment filled with explosives.

RUC officers were frequent targets of PIRA and other terrorist groups.

In early May 1987, the RUC received word that a mechanical digger had been stolen from a construction site in East Tyrone. An attack was pending, they knew. But where?

Police, on a nationwide search for the digger, soon discovered it at a seldom-used farmhouse about ten miles down the road from an RUC station at Loughgall in County Armagh. A team from 22 SAS was dispatched to Loughgall to monitor the farmhouse. The operators, in well-camouflaged observation posts, soon observed PIRA operatives bringing loads of explosives into the farmhouse and rigging the digger with a bomb.

British intelligence also listened in on a phone call between two PIRA commanders, who said PIRA was ready to strike. The commanders, lieutenants in the notorious East Tyrone Brigade, were known for daring attacks against the RUC and British military, including an attack on the RUC station in the Armagh months earlier. British commanders were determined not to let the East Tyrone Brigade carry out another such attack.

THE STRIKE

The SAS prepared an ambush. Code named Operation Judy, it involved a sixteen-man troop. Because they knew both the target and method of attack, the SAS and RUC quietly and secretly evacuated the police officers in Loughgall. They inserted their own operators, including sharpshooters, into the station.

The Loughgall police station, following the clash between SAS and PIRA operatives. A barrel-bomb left the station partially destroyed.

The PIRA plan, the British knew, was to crash their vehicles into the police station and toss in their barrel-bomb. But before they could do it, the SAS team planned to wipe them out in a furious field of fire.

The attack was scheduled for 7:20 on the night of May 8, 1987. The mechanical digger, along with PIRA operatives in a blue van, approached the police station as planned: the blue van charged toward the police station, and the digger slammed through the gate. Two East Tyrone Brigade terrorists began firing automatic rifles at the police station, and the SAS returned fire. The eight PIRA terrorists never had a prayer. During the exchange of gunfire, the barrel-bomb exploded, resulting in massive destruction to the police station.

By the time the smoke cleared, British army choppers had extracted the SAS team, leaving only the police detectives to clear up the scene and the dead bodies of the terrorists. Operation Judy had been a smashing success.

A NEW TARGET

Inside the ranks of the PIRA, the defeat at Loughgall paralyzed operations for nearly a year. Loughgall had to be avenged. But the PIRA abandoned the strategy of striking at police stations and military targets inside Northern Ireland. Instead, the PIRA would once again think large scale and grand. It wanted to bring about a major loss of life.

The target selected was remote and symbolic—the British fortress on Gibraltar, a British colony south of Spain. Gibraltar was one of the few remaining symbols of the grandeur of the historic British Empire. Unlike heavily defended police stations and government buildings in the British Isles, Gibraltar was viewed as a "soft target." Although a British military garrison was stationed there, its defenses were light.

Three of the PIRA's most dependable and capable operatives—Daniel McCann, Sean Savage, and Mairead Farrell—were assigned to bomb a ceremonial parade at Gibraltar on March 8, 1988. The daily parade attracted hundreds of tourists, pedestrians, schoolchildren, and other civilians. A powerful car bomb detonated near the parade, even half as powerful as the Loughgall device, could kill one hundred people and maim countless more.

The three PIRA master terrorists maintained a low profile as they prepared for the operation in Gibraltar. But local authorities grew suspicious of the three and contacted the MI6, Britain's foreign intelligence service, as well as the SAS. The British devised a plan to capture—or kill—the PIRA squad. It was code named Operation Flavius.

In March 1988, the PIRA began watching the target in Gibraltar. British agents observed a PIRA operative photographing the guardhouse and the ceremony. An attack, British officials feared, was about to take place. On March 3, sixteen SAS operators arrived in Gibraltar and Spain.

The ceremonial parade in Gibraltar attracts hundreds of onlookers daily. A bombing there would cause massive civilian casualties.

The SAS team knew that the PIRA operatives were probably heavily armed and equipped with explosives. They assumed the terrorists would use a remote-controlled car bomb to attack the parade.

THE STRIKE

On March 6, just before 3:00 P.M., British surveillance teams saw the three terrorists enter downtown Gibraltar. The three then walked back to the Spanish border, leaving a white car behind near the parade site. This was it, SAS team leaders assumed. The car contained a bomb, and the attack would come that day.

Along with the SAS team, local police officers drove toward the three terrorists with lights and sirens ablaze. The sound of sirens caused the three to stop in their tracks. Reportedly, McCann and Farrell spotted the SAS men, who were by then only eleven yards away. They attempted to resist arrest. An SAS operator opened fire, striking McCann. He was shot five more times and killed.

Farrell made a sudden move, reaching for what the operators thought was the bomb's detonator in her handbag. She, too, was cut down and killed by SAS fire. The SAS cornered Savage, as well. He refused to heed calls to raise his arms and surrender. Instead, he reached inside his field jacket. SAS operators didn't know if he was reaching for a weapon or a detonator. They shot him eighteen times, killing him.

But Operation Flavius remains one of the most controversial operations ever mounted by the British against Irish terrorism. It turned out that none of the three Irish operatives killed were armed at the time of the shootings. Nor were any detonators found. In fact, an investigation revealed that the white car did not have a single ounce of explosives in it.

Although the SAS had made a mistake (in an official inquiry, the SAS operators were cleared of any wrongdoing), the raid did achieve one important goal: 22 SAS, already feared and hated in Northern Ireland, became a legendary force that sent shivers down the spines of even the most zealous Irish terrorists. Operation Flavius became the SAS counterterrorist calling card.

WHO'S WHO AND
WHAT'S WHAT

Khalil al-Wazir (Abu Jihad): a top PLO leader from 1973 until his assassination in 1988

Mossad: Israel's foreign intelligence agency

night-vision glasses: electronic devices that allow military forces to detect and track targets at night. Night-vision glasses work by turning temperature readings into images.

Tunisia: a North African nation on the Mediterranean Sea. Most Tunisians speak Arabic and practice Islam. The Tunisian government has sometimes provided a safe haven for terrorist leaders, including Abu Jihad.

UNFINISHED BUSINESS: THE DEATH OF ABU JIHAD

The driver maneuvered the van through the twisting streets and frenzied traffic as though he had traveled the city all his life. The closer the van got to its target, the more focused the driver became. The men sitting inside the van were all quiet. Nobody spoke. No one dared utter a word in Hebrew, the language of their native Israel. After all, everyone in Tunis, the capital of Tunisa, spoke Arabic or French.

The driver glanced in his rearview mirror every few intersections to see what the other men were doing. Some held assault rifles against their chins. Others made sure silencers were snuggly fastened to their rifle barrels. One operator checked, rechecked, and then checked once again his silenced pistol. Another readied his video camera. If history was going to be made, it needed to be preserved on tape.

A busy street in Tunis, Tunisia, where Abu Jihad made his home

The van made its way toward the Sidi Bou Said section of town, where the rich and famous lived. The target was only minutes away. Opulent homes dotted the tree-lined street. The targeted house had a team of security men in plainclothes out front. They carried AK-47s and uttered into walkie-talkies. The driver knew this was the location. Truth time had arrived.

Other Israeli vehicles were already parked along the street, maintaining a close watch on the house. The drivers fired their engines when the van, one of several, arrived. Before the armed guards realized what was happening, silenced .22 and 9mm rounds entered the backs of their heads. This was the time of truth, indeed.

TERROR AND COUNTERTERROR

Khalil al-Wazir, known as Abu Jihad, had been Yasser Arafat's top military commander since April 1973. An Arafat loyalist who had guided PLO forces through some bloody times, Abu Jihad had been forced out of Beirut, Lebanon, and had moved to Tunis.

Israel had wanted Abu Jihad dead for some time. He was responsible for dozens of high-profile terrorist attacks that had killed hundreds of Israelis. But two operations had particularly enraged the

Yasser Arafat and his trusted commander Abu Jihad *(right)*

Israelis. In 1985 Abu Jihad had sent more than forty terrorists toward the Israeli shore by boat. The terrorists planned to land on a beach south of Tel Aviv, seize a bus, and drive it into Israel's sprawling Defense Ministry compound. They also planned to assassinate Israeli defense minister Yitzhak Rabin. But the Israeli navy caught the Palestinian boat at sea and killed or captured all the terrorists before they could land on the Israeli coast.

The next operation came in 1988, when Jihad sent a terrorist squad to attack an Israeli nuclear plant in Dimona, in Israel's Negev Desert. The attack did not succeed, but in the course of the operation, the terrorists seized a bus full of women who worked at the plant. Israeli soldiers saved the women in a spectacular rescue operation. The thwarted attack on the nuclear plant was the final straw. Israeli commanders wanted Jihad dead. They simply needed to work out the details.

Israeli forces spring into action to rescue a bus full of workers held by Palestinian terrorists in 1988.

Throughout early April 1988, the Mossad, Israeli's foreign spy agency, had dispatched teams of agents—men and women and all with European passports—to Tunis to lay the groundwork for the assassination. The Mossad agents rented vehicles, took hotel rooms, and worked out other details of the attack. The assault force would be made up of operators from Sayeret Mat'kal and Flotilla 13. The task force would travel to the coast of Tunis on Israeli navy missile boats. Aircraft would fly overhead to provide support in case the commandos got in trouble.

THE STRIKE

Just after midnight on April 16, 1988, Israeli *commanders waited on the missile boats anchored offshore. They scanned the Tunisian coastline through high-powered binoculars.*

FLOTILLA 13

Counterterrorist units, regardless of their size, equipment, or budget, are measured by only one standard—their experience. Few units in the world have more experience than Israel's Flotilla 13.

On paper, Flotilla 13 is not a counterterrorist unit. It is the special warfare unit of the Israeli navy. It focuses on secret operations against enemy ships and conventional military targets. In 1948, during Israel's war for independence, Flotilla 13 destroyed the flagship (ship that carries the commander) of the Egyptian navy. During the Six-Day War in 1967, the unit staged daring yet unsuccessful raids against Egyptian and Syrian ports. In 1973, during the Yom Kippur War, Flotilla 13 destroyed scores of Soviet-supplied missile boats in the Egyptian Red Sea Fleet.

During the 1970s, the flotilla began targeting Palestinian terrorists. Between 1979 and 1982, it carried out more than one thousand missions against Palestinian terrorist bases along the Lebanese coast. Sometimes the missions were small-scale operations—ambushing trucks carrying ammunition and weapons. In other raids, the flotilla destroyed terrorist facilities, killed scores of terrorists, and carried off file cabinets' worth of intelligence materials.

Sometimes, Flotilla 13's missions take it far from Israel's shores, as with the raid to assassinate Abu Jihad in Tunis. Most of the unit's operations remain state secrets of the highest order. ■

Major General Ehud Barak, head of Israeli military intelligence, led the operation.

Without much talk or fanfare, the missile boats' crew tossed several inflatable rubber boats into the dark, curling waves. Along with their night-vision gear, packs of equipment, and silenced weapons, the operators lowered themselves one by one into the bobbing craft. Mossad agents waited onshore near rented vans. They scanned the darkened Mediterranean Sea through high-powered night-vision glasses, searching for the outlines of the approaching boats.

Without a word spoken—especially not in Hebrew—the commandos coming in from the sea hooked up with their escorts on the beach and embarked into the twisting and honking late-night traffic in Tunis. The caravan of rented vehicles sliced through the

Under the command of Major General Ehud Barak *(above)*, the operation against Abu Jihad was a stunning success.

hillside roads and city thoroughfares toward the posh villas of Sidi Bou Said, a favorite neighborhood of PLO leadership living in Tunis. Plainclothes Palestinian security teams patrolled the streets of the fancy suburb. Tunisian police officers routinely drove by the homes of high-ranking PLO commanders to assure their safety.

The commandos, divided into four attack squads, carried enough firepower to hold off a brigade of such troops. More important, hovering more than forty-thousand feet above Tunis, an Israeli air force plane was busy monitoring and jamming the radio and telephone frequencies used by the Tunisian and Palestinian security forces.

The hit squad wanted to kill Jihad as he slept, not in a shootout. At 2:30 A.M., the lights inside the second-floor bedroom in Abu Jihad's villa went off. The operators went into action. Emerging from vans parked near the villa, the commandos went to work in precise fashion. They shot several Palestinian and Tunisian sentries with silenced gunfire and blew the iron gates protecting the home off their hinges with small explosives.

Entering the villa, the operators moved quickly and silently, racing up the marble stairway in rubber-soled boots. The commandos entered Abu Jihad's bedroom and found him asleep next to his wife. He was cut down by a flurry of about seventy bullets. His wife was not killed. The entire operation was videotaped.

The assassination of Abu Jihad was a marvel of efficiency and planning. The target had been killed, and the assault teams, along with their support force, all snuck out of Tunis long before the befuddled Tunisian security officials knew what had happened.

WHO'S WHO AND
WHAT'S WHAT

Ahmed Jibril: founder and commander of the Popular Front for the Liberation of Palestine General Command

Golani Brigade: A unit of special operators in the Israel Defense Forces

intifada: a large-scale Palestinian uprising, mostly carried out by civilians rather than by terrorist factions

Israel Defense Forces: Israel's primary security and military organization

occupied territories: the West Bank and Gaza Strip, areas adjacent to Israel and controlled by Israel since the Six-Day War in 1967. The territories are primarily home to Palestinians. Within the territories, a body called the Palestinian Authority handles local governance.

Popular Front for the Liberation of Palestine General Command (PFLP-GC): a terrorist group founded in 1968 by Ahmed Jibril and supported by Syria and Iran

THE DOGS OF WAR: OPERATION BLUE AND BROWN

The light show inside the cave *was awe inspiring and paralyzing. In complete and absolute darkness, the tracer ammunition erupted from a hundred assault rifles and light machine guns. The shooters, wearing night-vision goggles, flinched in the flickering brightness. The fusillade of gunfire competed with thin red light beams from the laser sights on the operators' weapons as they advanced slowly through the cave.*

The operators were wary of trip wires that would set off booby traps and other explosive devices. Their survival depended on how fast they killed the dozens of terrorists entrenched in their fortified underground positions. Amid the smoke, the operators pushed into a wall of fire, knowing they had to get the job done and get back to the rendezvous point (meeting place) for the transport back home.

TERROR AND COUNTERTERROR

Ahmed Jibril was a terrorist mastermind whom the state of Israel wanted dead. The wily leader of the Popular Front for the Liberation of Palestine General Command (PFLP-GC) had, in a twenty-year career, taken the art of terror and bloodshed to a new level. Jibril targeted the most helpless and innocent of victims. His first operation was an ambush in northern Israel. His operatives had fired an antitank rocket at a school bus filled with toddlers.

Yet Jibril's true passion was technical terrorism—the nuts and bolts of using new technology to achieve enormous body counts. Jibril's primary target was Israel's national airline, El Al, and foreign airlines that traveled

Ahmed Jibril oversaw a vast terror complex.

to Israel. In February 1970, Jibril had used altimeter bombs—triggered by changes in air pressure—in simultaneous attacks against Swissair and Austrian Airlines planes en route to Tel Aviv. The Swissair jet exploded over the Alps. Everyone on board was killed. The Austrian Airlines jet miraculously made a safe landing despite the bombing. Over the course of the next eighteen years, Jibril attempted to plant altimeter bombs on at least a dozen El Al jets, but El Al security foiled each attempt.

On November 25, 1987, Jibril sent a terrorist from Lebanon into Israel on a motorized hang glider. The terrorist's target was an apartment house in the northern Israeli town of Ma'alot. He was supposed to shoot and kill everyone inside. Yet when he crossed over from southern Lebanon and landed in northern Israel, he strayed from his mission and proceeded to launch a strike against a nearby military camp. He charged into the base with weapons ablaze. He killed six soldiers and wounded nearly one hundred more before being cut down by seventy-five bullets.

El Al practices the tightest security measures possible to protect its passengers from terrorist attack.

The next day, Palestinians in the West Bank and Gaza Strip (the occupied territories) began to riot in support of the gunman. More riots soon erupted. The rioting and subsequent violence became known as the intifada, or uprising. Israeli intelligence blamed the uprising on Jibril.

Jibril next plotted to blow a U.S. airliner out of the sky. He sent his top operatives to Germany to plan the bombing, but German security

Many young people joined the intifada in the Gaza Strip.

agents arrested them. Still, Jibril continued plotting, planning to hit a U.S. plane flying through London's Heathrow Airport.

Jibril had to be stopped. The Israel Defense Forces (IDF) chief of staff, Lieutenant General Dan Shomron, a veteran of previous counterterrorist raids, gave the green light for his men to take out Jibril.

Jibril shared his time between his headquarters in Damascus, Syria, and a unique PFLP-GC command and training center in the village of al-Na'amah, about fifteen miles south of Beirut, Lebanon, and three miles inland from the Mediterranean coast. The facility consisted of several two- and three-story buildings. It was hemmed in by nearby hills and a series of natural caves and ravines, used by Jibril to store weapons and house fighters. About 150 men and women served at the al-Na'amah camp, including Jibril's elite special operations force known as the Sabra and Shatilla Battalion.

The caves and buildings were connected by a series of underground tunnels, which allowed the facility to function even under heavy bombardment. The tunnels also ran to the center of the complex—Jibril's personal underground command and control facility and living quarters, situated inside a steel-encased bunker. Getting Jibril would not be easy. The target was as hardened as they came.

The task force commander, Lieutenant Colonel Amir Meital, was a top-notch officer. He was careful, daring, and cool under fire. His infantrymen, members of Israel's Golani Brigade, would approach from the sea, joined by the elite naval commandos of Flotilla 13. The Golani infantrymen wore brown berets, while the naval commandos wore blue berets. So the mission was code named Operation Blue and Brown. It would strike at four targets:

- Jibril's underground headquarters
- Six caves that served as the living quarters for the Sabra and Shatilla Battalion
- The al-Na'amah training facility
- The base's antiaircraft defenses, consisting of 23mm cannons and shoulder-fired surface-to-air missiles

Operation Blue and Brown was as risky as they come—especially hitting the first two targets, which were almost completely underground. To minimize risk to the soldiers, the IDF planned to use dogs, primarily rottweilers, strapped with explosive packs to be detonated by remote control. The tactic was bold, but if the underground maze was not cleared of enemy fighters before the commandos entered it, the operation could be a suicide mission, the commanders feared.

Israel's defense minister Yitzhak Rabin and much of the IDF general staff would monitor and coordinate the operation from the IDF's underground command and control facility in Tel Aviv. Israeli Air Force fighter-bomber squadrons would be nearby, in the skies over Lebanon, ready to hammer the al-Na'amah camp and nearby roads should the attack force find itself in trouble. The jets would also attack any men the Palestinians or Syrians tried to send in as reinforcements. The air force's elite rescue unit, Unit 669, was also on call, along with its fleet of heavy-duty choppers.

For weeks the Golani infantrymen and naval commandos trained in northern Israel, using a model of the al-Na'amah facility. The infantrymen practiced assaulting a series of mock targets in complete darkness, using only their night-vision goggles to see and laser-aiming

The Israeli air force provided air cover for Operation Brown and Blue.

devices fitted to their assault rifles. D-day for the operation was December 8, 1988—the first anniversary of the outbreak of the intifada.

THE STRIKE

The first naval commandos emerged from the Mediterranean surf along the Lebanese coast at 9:15 P.M. on December 8, 1988. After securing the landing zone, they ordered in a small armada of inflatable boats carrying the Golani task force and its dogs. Then both the naval and infantry commandos began the two-mile march toward al-Na'amah.

The march was done in silence and hurriedly. The operators pushed their legs and those of their dogs to the limit. Each commando carried more than sixty-pounds of gear, including antitank rockets and loads of ammo, in rucksacks bursting at the seams. Cold winter winds whipped harshly from mountains to the north and east.

By 2:45 A.M., the commandos had reached al-Na'amah. First, the naval commandos struck the PFLP-GC sentries protecting the facility. They used silenced weapons to kill the sentries, then spread out through the camp. The moment the attack began, an alarm sounded in the base, and Jibril's underground bunker was reinforced and sealed off with steel doors. A brutal firefight began at the entrance to the bunker.

The naval commander then sent several dogs into the tunnels.

They galloped in, only to disintegrate in a blinding explosive flash when a commando triggered the remote-controlled bombs they carried. Other dogs were confused and disoriented by the gunfire. Some were shot by Palestinians, who aimed at their explosive packs. Others were captured and later killed by Jibril's men. The Israeli plan to use dogs to secure the tunnels had not worked.

A pitched battle began in the darkness. The naval commandos and Golani operators fired antitank rockets at the bunker doors. But the armor-piercing rockets simply exploded against the mighty steel doors without causing any damage. Demolitions experts, armed with satchels full of explosives, attempted to place their loads at strategic points near the steel door. But the Palestinian fire was too intense.

As the battle for the bunker continued, Lieutenant Colonel Meital proceeded toward the six earthen caves where the PFLP-GC garrison slept. The caves were at the far end of the camp, so by the time Meital's men struck, the terrorists had already readied their defenses. The battle inside the caves was close-up and brutal. Muzzle flashes and explosions lit up the darkness. Slowly, the Golani infantrymen advanced far enough to engage the Palestinians in hand-to-hand combat. The cries of the wounded were almost as loud as the bursts of 5.56mm fire. Injured infantrymen were carried out of the cave to makeshift evacuation centers. The cave floor became slippery with the blood of those who had been shot.

Lieutenant Colonel Meital would be the next casualty. As he spoke on the radio summoning in reinforcements, a bullet sliced through his helmet, killing the young commander instantly. The unit doctor rushing to help him was also cut down and critically injured by a burst of terrorist machine-gun fire.

With Meital dead, the naval commando commander took charge. But the operation was not looking hopeful. Daylight was only an hour away. The time to safely evacuate the soldiers, along with the wounded and dead, was quickly dwindling. So the naval commander summoned in a fleet of rescue choppers and ordered his men to evacuate. As the Israeli soldiers retreated, fighters, bombers, and helicopter gunships unleashed a relentless barrage of cannon and missile fire to protect them.

As the evacuation helicopters rushed toward al-Na'amah, the

naval commander ordered his men to blow up the three-story building directly above Jibril's bunker. He hoped the collapsing structure would trap Jibril inside. The bright, eye-searing flash of the explosion was followed by an eardrum-splitting thud.

The blast was ideal cover for the retreat, but something was amiss. A head count revealed that four Israelis were missing. The naval and Golani commandos began calling to the missing men on an emergency radio frequency. They even used bullhorns, but the four failed to respond. As it turned out, the men were only five hundred feet from the evacuation zone, but they were pinned down by terrorist fire. And they were unable to respond because their radio had been damaged by shrapnel.

The IDF refuses to leave a soldier on the battlefield—dead or alive. So the commanders would not abandon the missing infantrymen. As the naval and Golani commandos were evacuated, Lieutenant General Shomron sent in additional rescue personnel. For three hours, the four men held off nearly one hundred PFLP-GC terrorists. Finally, the men managed to fix their radio and send their location to rescue helicopters that hovered nearby. In a dramatic rescue, the four men were plucked and carried to safety on the landing skids of two Cobra gunships. As the choppers flew out of the kill zone, the bodies of scores of terrorists were evident amid the smoke and fire.

Operation Blue and Brown was one of the most ambitious counterterrorist operations ever staged. The death toll among Jibril's men was staggering. Nearly one hundred terrorists were believed to have been killed that night. Dozens more had been critically wounded. Jibril's entire underground complex was exposed, and much of it was destroyed. The terrorist chieftain survived, however. He reportedly remained inside his bunker for sixteen hours after the last shots were fired.

Yet for all its gusto and imagination, the raid was a failure in the long run. Back in Israel, as friends, family, and comrades buried Lieutenant Colonel Meital, Ahmed Jibril gave a press conference. He held an assault rifle abandoned by a wounded Golani soldier and vowed revenge. Less than two weeks later, on the night of December 21, 1988, Pan Am Flight 103 blew up over Lockerbie, Scotland, killing 259 people on the aircraft and 11 on the ground. Ahmed Jibril was directly involved in the crime.

Abdullah Ocalan: leader of the Kurdistan Workers Party since 1978

communism: a social and political philosophy in which property is owned by the whole community rather than by individuals. The community also controls the means for producing and distributing goods (such as crops and steel).

Kurdistan Workers Party (Partia Karkaren Kurdistan, or PKK): a Kurdish nationalist political and terrorist organization that has been waging war against the Turkish government since 1984. In 2002 the PKK changed its name to the Congress for Freedom and Democracy in Kurdistan.

Kurds: an ethnic group whose historic homeland stretches across parts of Turkey, Iraq, and Iran. The Kurds have been fighting for an independent nation since the mid-twentieth century.

Turkey: a country located between Europe and the Middle East, with a large Kurdish population

OUT OF AFRICA:
THE KIDNAPPING OF
ABDULLAH OCALAN

The operators, the best men in the Turkish armed forces and intelligence services, practiced the takedown in a desolate part of Istanbul, Turkey. The training ground, a slum, had been the squad's home base for nearly three months. They had trained virtually around the clock. Every aspect of the complex operation was critiqued, corrected, and carried out again and again until each segment was foolproof.

Secret service vans would follow the target as he left the safe house by car. At an intersection, the vans would box in the target's car. Operators would emerge from the vans, ready to blow away anyone who resisted. The target would be subdued, tossed into an awaiting getaway car, and placed on an aircraft within twenty minutes of capture. The operators, black masks covering their faces, would carry MP5 submachine guns, to be used only as a last resort.

Snatching a human target was risky, especially when the target had to be picked up in a foreign country. A million and one things could go wrong. But this mission was of paramount national importance. There would be no second chances—only regret if the operation failed. There could be no mistakes. Only success!

As the cold February winds raced in from the mountains to the north and east, the unit fine-tuned its assault plan until it was flawless. With a little luck, the most wanted man in the country would soon be in jail. With a little luck, one of the bloodiest periods in the country's history was about to end. Snatching the man was that important. That man was Abdullah Ocalan.

TERROR AND COUNTERTERROR | Abdullah Ocalan is

Kurdish. The Kurds are an ethnic group whose historic homeland is in parts of modern-day Turkey, Iraq, and Iran. Ocalan had been born in 1948 in the Kurdish village of Omerli in eastern Turkey. He grew up to become a Kurdish leader. He believed in his people's right to an independent homeland, and he rallied others to protest for Kurdish rights.

In 1978 Ocalan created the Kurdistan Workers Party (Partia Karkaren Kurdistan in Kurdish, or PKK). The PKK is an extremist group

Abdullah Ocalan greets PKK fighters at a training camp in Lebanon.

that uses murder and violence to fight for Kurdish rights and independence. In addition, Ocalan embraced the communist philosophy, which involves government control of all businesses and property. Ocalan dreamed of starting a communist revolution inside Turkey.

At training camps in Lebanon and Syria, thousands of PKK operatives learned the art of assassination, hijacking, and bombing. Some PKK terrorists attacked targets in Turkey. Others were sent to Western Europe—primarily Germany—where they targeted Turkish diplomats, embassies, and airline offices. In all, PKK attacks killed more than thirty-five thousand Turks (including Kurds who didn't support the group's goals or methods). In turn, the Turkish government cracked down on PKK

PKK fighters drill and exercise at a Lebanese camp.

fighters, arresting and killing thousands of Kurds and restricting the rights of Kurdish people.

The violence raged for nearly twenty years. By 1998 Turkey had had enough. It threatened to invade northern Syria if Syria continued to allow the PKK to operate there. Syria buckled to Turkish pressure. It closed down PKK facilities inside its borders and expelled Ocalan.

Ocalan first attempted to find safe haven in Russia, part of the former Soviet Union. The Soviets had once generously supplied the PKK with weapons and money. But the Russians, under intense Turkish and U.S. pressure, refused to admit him. Ocalan fled to Italy and then Greece, a Turkish enemy.

The Greeks realized that openly supporting the most wanted man in Turkey risked embroiling the eastern Mediterranean region in full-scale war. So the Greeks flew Ocalan to their embassy in Nairobi, Kenya. The Greek government then tried to find a country in Africa willing to harbor the Kurdish leader. The Greeks hoped Turkey would never learn about its support for Ocalan. His move to Nairobi was done under a blanket of absolute secrecy.

But U.S. and Israeli agents tipped off the Turks to Ocalan's whereabouts. The Turks decided to snatch him from Nairobi using their top-secret counterterrorist force, the Burgundy Berets. They were operating under great time pressure—Ocalan could leave Kenya at any moment.

The Turks did not want to assassinate Ocalan. Killing him without the benefit of questioning and a trial would turn the fifty-one-year-old symbol of Kurdish independence into a martyr. Ocalan had to be captured. He needed to be brought back to Turkey, where he could stand trial and eventually be punished for his crimes.

THE STRIKE

Turkish intelligence agents flew to Nairobi in 1999 from airports throughout the Middle East. They began to monitor the Greek embassy in downtown Nairobi. They learned that Ocalan was planning to move to the home of a Greek ambassador in a secluded part of town, then fly to the Netherlands.

Burgundy Berets arrived in Nairobi too. Operating out of the Turkish embassy there, they waited in the city's bustling streets, watching for Ocalan to leave the Greek embassy. When he did, the commandos sprang into action. Their fleet of rented vans boxed Ocalan in and kept his vehicle from escaping. Black masks covering their faces, the operators moved in a flash of speed and daunting

A Turkish guard watches Ocalan on the flight back to Turkey.

power. They pulled the Kurdish terrorist leader from his vehicle, quickly blindfolding him and binding his hands. They tossed him into a van heading for Nairobi's international airport.

Within a half hour of being seized, Ocalan was leaving Kenya for Turkey on a French-built jet. The man responsible for so much bloodshed and destruction, the warrior whose mustached face had become a symbol of the PKK reign of terror, was in shackles, surrounded by Turkish commandos. The following morning, a blindfolded Ocalan, his hands cuffed in front of his waist, was videotaped for Turkish TV, standing beside a gigantic Turkish flag.

Kurds throughout Europe violently protested Ocalan's arrest. PKK supporters stormed Turkish embassies in Berlin, Paris, Rome, and the Netherlands. But Ocalan was brought to justice. In the end, he was convicted on four hundred counts of treason, murder, terror, and violence against the Turkish state. He was eventually sentenced to life behind bars.

Abdullah Ocalan sits behind bulletproof glass and under heavy guard during his trial in May 1999.

The capture of Abdullah Ocalan was a brilliant operation that forever improved Turkey's ability to safeguard its citizens. The Turks had been after Ocalan since 1980. The operation to seize him lasted just twelve days.

Australia: a nation on an island continent between the South Pacific Ocean and the Indian Ocean. It is a member of the U.S.-led coalition to defeat terrorist fighters in Afghanistan.

coalition: a group of nations, led by the United States, that came together to fight terrorists in Afghanistan

Marinejægerkommandos: Norway's naval commando unit

Operation Anaconda: a mission to flush out al-Qaeda leaders from caves in southeastern Afghanistan

Operation Enduring Freedom: the U.S.-led war on terrorism in Afghanistan

special operations forces: various commando units within the U.S. military. Examples include the army's Special Forces and Delta Force and the navy's SEALs. Other nations also maintain special operations forces.

THE SNAKE'S VENOM:
OPERATION ANACONDA

he temperature in the mountains was bone-chilling. The
ice- and snow-covered rocks were treacherous. But the Australian
operators strutted on, determined not to allow the elements—or al-
Qaeda—to interfere with their plans. An MH-47 chopper had dropped
them off just after sunset in the mountains of eastern Afghanistan. The
rest of the terrain was to be covered on foot.

The line of operators from Australia's Special Air Service
Regiment, or SASR, moved quickly along the ridgeline. Standing in
one place for too long was dangerous in Afghanistan, especially so
close to the Pakistani border, where the terrorists were strongest. Each

Australia joined the United States in its attack on the Taliban and
al-Qaeda in 2001. Here, Australian air force jets train over the
Australian outback.

man carried just enough ammunition and equipment to keep him alive in the mountains for several days of fighting.

On this moonless night, the SASR was going to kill the enemy as it ran away from a massive U.S.-led air strike. Soldiers and commandos from several dozen countries had joined the United States in its campaign against al-Qaeda. This was a true world war.

The operators reached the place that the mission commander had circled in red on the map. From a ridge overlooking an ancient trail, the operators waited for the air strikes to slow down. Through their night-vision goggles, they watched for figures to emerge from their hiding spots, attempting to escape toward neighboring Pakistan.

TERROR AND COUNTERTERROR | When the United

States launched its international war on terrorism in Afghanistan in 2001—Operation Enduring Freedom—two things were blatantly clear. First, the war would be a lengthy and difficult struggle. Afghanistan would be only the first theater of operations in a global antiterror campaign. Second, special operations forces would play an all-important role in the destruction of al-Qaeda and the hunt for its leader, Osama bin Laden. Bin Laden was the mastermind behind the 2001 terrorist attacks in the United States.

The first U.S. troops to arrive in Afghanistan were special operations units: the army's Special Forces, Delta Force, and Special Operations Aviation Regiment; the air force's Special Operations Wing; and the navy's SEALs. These units worked independently, far behind enemy lines. They were charged with creating an atmosphere that would cripple the terrorists—an atmosphere of fear. Operating at night, with high-tech night-vision and surveillance gear, special operations units denied the terrorists safety in the darkness and placed them under constant pressure. In caves and remote mountain villages, they hunted down al-Qaeda terrorists and their supporters.

The special operations effort was not solely a U.S. endeavor, however. The United States had put together a coalition of allied countries, and many of these countries sent special troops to Afghanistan. Britain sent troops from its elite 22 SAS regiment and its Royal Marines Special Boat Service. Australia and New Zealand sent in their Special Air Service forces. Canada sent operators from its Joint Task Force Two. Germany sent its KSK force. Norway sent its Marinejægerkommandos (naval hunters), as did Denmark.

Operation Enduring Freedom was an initial success. But by spring 2002—six months after the September 11, 2001, attacks—Osama bin Laden and much of the al-Qaeda leadership had still not been caught. Coalition commanders realized they needed to undertake a major offensive against the terrorists in Afghanistan. The coalition had to flush the al-Qaeda leadership from its shelter of caves in the mountains of southeastern Afghanistan. That campaign became known as Operation Anaconda.

A British Royal Marine climbs a hill in southeastern Afghanistan.

THE STRIKE | Operation Anaconda began on the night of March 1, 2002. The targeted terrain, at an altitude of eight thousand to twelve

HUNTERS FROM THE FJORDS

The U.S.-led war against terrorism in Afghanistan was truly an international campaign—especially in the special operations arena. Units from a dozen different nations took part in the campaign. One of the most famous was Norway's Marinejægerkommandos.

The Marinejægerkommandos, established in 1968, specialize in reconnaissance, intelligence gathering, and operations deep behind enemy lines. They operate in small units consisting of two to twelve men. Altogether, the unit has nearly two hundred men.

For nearly fifty years, Norway's naval hunters have served as the razor's edge of naval special operations in Europe. When the United States needed help in Afghanistan, Norway responded to the challenge—and so did the hunters. ■

thousand feet, was perhaps the roughest mountain stretch in the world. On good days, the temperature was well below freezing. On bad days—and there were always bad days—the temperature was below zero.

The operation involved two thousand coalition troops. Half of them were paratroopers from the U.S. Army's 101st Airborne Division and infantrymen from the 10th Mountain Division. Friendly Afghan troops would support the operation. The mission plan was simple: Air forces and ground units would hammer the terrorist safe havens with relentless shelling and bombing. Once the caves were destroyed, the terrorists would flee. Special operations units would then strike the fleeing terrorists from the air and ambush them on the ground.

The operation went as planned. During the shelling and bombing, special units positioned themselves at key mountain paths and cave networks. Once the al-Qaeda fighters emerged from their damaged caves, special operators engaged them. Some terrorists fled into surrounding homes and villages. Special operators pursued them. There were vicious firefights, one in the Shah-e-kot Valley.

Operation Anaconda lasted for nearly two weeks. In the end, the fighting was one-sided and unforgiving. The coalition's special operators—expert shots and masters at fast and mobile warfare—were just too strong for al-Qaeda. About eight hundred terrorists were killed. Their weapons depots, supply routes, and ability to move about freely were completely wiped out.

U.S. forces destroy more than one million rounds of Afghan ammunition and fuel, captured during raids on terrorist hideouts in southeastern Afghanistan.

One of the unstated objectives of Operation Anaconda had been the capture or killing of Osama bin Laden. The coalition knew it had gotten close to the terrorist leader. It was possible that he had even been wounded in the fighting. But bin Laden had not been killed. By 2004 his whereabouts remained unknown. And the war against terrorism continued.

WHO'S WHO AND
WHAT'S WHAT

Central Intelligence Agency: the U.S. agency that gathers information about foreign governments and enemies

Hamburg Cell: the group of al-Qaeda terrorists, operating from Hamburg, Germany, who planned and carried out the September 11, 2001, attacks

Pakistan: a nation in southern Asia. Almost all Pakistanis are Muslims.

Ramzi Binalshibh: an al-Qaeda operative who was heavily involved in planning the September 11, 2001, attacks in the United States

the West: the democratic nations of Europe and North America

SUNRISE IN KARACHI:
THE ARREST OF
RAMZI BINALSHIBH

The dozen or so vans moved into the Karachi neighborhood in a slow procession. The beat-up Fiat and Toyota vans were nondescript. They blended into the dusty squalor brilliantly. Six men rode in each van, making their way into the crowded Pakistani slum. Each man was armed with an AK-47. Walkie-talkies linked the team to the overall commander in the lead van. That was where the Americans were.

The men slid their AK-47s inside their clothing and emerged from the vans in different spots around the edge of the targeted apartment building. They would try to stop any possible escape and then close the circle slowly but surely around their prey. The men were experts.

Karachi, Pakistan, is a crowded city, where camels and motor vehicles compete for space in the bustling streets.

But for men about to launch a surprise raid against one of the most wanted terrorists in the world, the mood was shockingly ordinary. The operators didn't wear helmets, vests, or other protective gear. Instead, they wore traditional Pakistani blouses and pants. Most didn't even wear shoes. They wore sandals, trying to look like average Pakistani citizens. But the prey was no ordinary man, and the team, as much as they tried to fit in, were the ones who stuck out. In a climate where only members of the same clan (extended family) are trusted, the new faces walking around the building were suspicious.

Suddenly, gunfire erupted. The concrete inside the narrow alleyways was chewed up into a cloud of dust and debris. Screams of women filled the street. Babies cried, and the innocent scurried for cover. The battle had only just begun.

TERROR AND COUNTERTERROR

When nineteen al-Qaeda hijackers struck the United States on September 11, 2001, the men who had dispatched them became wanted men. U.S. president George W. Bush said the masterminds behind the attacks were wanted dead or alive, but the U.S. government really wanted them alive. Dead men, after

President Bush meets with firefighters and rescue workers outside the Pentagon in Washington, D.C., one day after terrorists crashed an airplane into the building.

all, do not tell any tales, and intelligence is the most important tool that governments have when combating an invisible enemy such as al-Qaeda. Men with details of terrorist cells, safe houses, and, most importantly, future plans were too valuable to be killed. They had to be captured alive so they could be questioned and persuaded to reveal information.

In the al-Qaeda roster of all-stars, Ramzi Binalshibh was a Hall of Famer. The thirty-year-old Yemeni-born bin Laden disciple had been a key commander in the Hamburg Cell, the secret core of terrorists who plotted and planned the September 11 attacks from Hamburg, Germany. In many ways, Binalshibh had been the twentieth hijacker on September

Ramzi Binalshibh has been called the "twentieth hijacker."

11. He had studied flight in Germany and had plans to come to the United States with the rest of the plotters, but he was denied a visa (a document allowing a foreigner to enter a county legally). Binalshibh had also been the coordinator who sent instructions back and forth between al-Qaeda commanders in Pakistan and Afghanistan and terrorists in Europe. He was the only one who attended both key planning sessions for the operation—one in Malaysia and the other in Spain.

Following 9/11, as U.S. troops in Afghanistan cleared out caves and questioned prisoners, one name kept reappearing: Ramzi Binalshibh. The "twentieth hijacker" had been promoted following the success of the bloody operation in the United States. He became a key al-Qaeda officer and commander. He was also on the run.

Binalshibh became one of the most wanted men on earth. Photos showing his long face and shabby beard were distributed to intelligence and law enforcement services around the world. For the United States, ending Binalshibh's career was a number one priority. There were a million places—from Saudi Arabia to the Sudan—where Binalshibh could be hiding. But most U.S. intelligence officials thought he was hiding in Pakistan.

Pakistan was an ally of the United States in the war against terror—but only on paper. Many of the 151 million people in Pakistan—a very poor nation—support Osama bin Laden's war against the West. Most Pakistanis embrace the Islamic religion. The United States, in their eyes, is evil. U.S. leaders knew that many Pakistanis would be willing to provide a safe haven to a man who had played a pivotal role in the 9/11 attacks.

On the night of September 10, 2002, U.S. intelligence units inside Pakistan intercepted a telephone call from a Karachi slum. The man on the line was Ramzi Binalshibh. Central Intelligence Agency (CIA) teams tracked the call to a five-story building in southern Karachi, in a

THE ROLLS-ROYCE OF KILLING TOOLS: THE HECKLER AND KOCH MP5

From U.S. Secret Service agents protecting the president to special operators fighting terrorists in Pakistan to police special response teams, one weapon is standard: the ever-reliable, compact, sturdy, and accurate Heckler and Koch MP5 9mm submachine gun. The world's top police and special operations units have come to rely upon the sleek, steel, German-made weapon.

The MP5 was first produced in the 1960s. It was originally designed as an all-purpose submachine gun for use by police officers and border guards in West Germany. It soon became the weapon of choice for special operations units worldwide. In 1980, after Britain's 22 SAS operators were seen negotiating the outer walls of the Iranian embassy in London cradling MP5s, the international tactical community

The Heckler and Koch MP5 submachine gun

was hooked. With few exceptions, the weapon can be found in the hands of security and special operations units in every country of the world.

In 2004 Heckler and Koch produced more than 120 variants of the original MP5, ranging from standard models to specialized weapons with built-in silencers. One MP5 even fits inside a briefcase. ■

neighborhood known to be an al-Qaeda stronghold. The "twentieth hijacker" was within their grasp.

U.S. operatives inside Pakistan wanted to be the ones to seize Binalshibh, but Pakistan's Inter-Service Intelligence (ISI) agency would have none of it. The ISI wanted to show the locals—especially pro–bin Laden militants—that they were a force to be reckoned with. A thirty-man ISI special operations team was assembled to snare Binalshibh. The Americans would be allowed to come along for the ride.

Storming the building at night was considered too dangerous. The five-story apartment building housing Binalshibh was full of trapdoors and terraces that could be used as hiding places. An al-Qaeda operative with a night-vision scope could, in a gun battle, kill every member of the ISI team and disappear before morning's first light. So the operation would take place in daylight.

THE STRIKE

The agents entered the neighborhood under cover of
*darkness. They sat at local cafés sipping tea and chain-smoking
cigarettes, all the while observing the scene. There was nothing high-
tech about ISI operations. No night-vision goggles, no body armor. The
radios they carried were twenty years old.*

*At 9:30 A.M. on September 11, 2002, an ISI advance team
arrested two men as they left the targeted building. Al-Qaeda
lookouts saw the arrest. The terrorists grabbed their weapons and
opted to fight rather than flee. The gunfire was hellacious. The
terrorists threw hand grenades at the rest of the ISI team, who were
by then taking defensive positions around the building. The U.S.
agents raced out of their vans and joined the fight. The ISI team was
flabbergasted. This was no ordinary apartment block in downtown
Karachi. This was a fortress.*

*For nearly an hour, the gunfire ate away at the concrete facades
of the neighborhood. The smoke and dust were suffocating. Civilians
hit by stray gunfire crawled to safety. Karachi police officers arrived
but were pinned down by terrorist snipers on the building's roof. The
ISI agents refused to back off. They were determined not to leave until
they had their man, dead or alive.*

The men fought street to street. The ISI team slowly advanced to the building's entrance and stairway. They then fought room to room. During a brief lull in the fighting, the ISI commander, using a bullhorn, pleaded with the men inside to surrender. The only response received was "Allahu akbar"—"God is great" in Arabic. The battle continued.

Although several ISI agents were wounded by gunfire, others pushed on to the targeted residence. Midday, as the international media arrived to report from the battle, ISI agents and Karachi police officers brought out a blindfolded man. "We got him," CIA operatives yelled into their cell phones, trying to be heard amid the gunfire still blazing and the screams of locals demanding that Binalshibh be released. It was a great victory in the war against terror.

As he was led away, Ramzi Binalshibh was defiant, yelling out militant slogans and trying to raise his shackled fists. But defiance soon waned to a whimper, and the Americans rushed Binalshibh out of Pakistan. He was taken to an undisclosed location for interrogation, where he remains in U.S. custody.

ISI agents hold a blindfolded Binalshibh after his dramatic capture in 2002. (He was still in U.S. custody in 2004.)

EPILOGUE

| ISLAMIC TERROR | The United States and other nations continue to wage war on Islamic terror on several fronts. In Afghanistan a U.S.-led coalition destroyed the Taliban and attacked al-Qaeda's top commanders. The coalition continues to pursue al-Qaeda leaders in Afghanistan, Pakistan, European countries, and the United States.

| ISRAEL AND THE PALESTINIANS | The Israeli-Palestinian conflict continues to rage in the Middle East. The PLO continues to operate as an umbrella group for the Palestinian cause.

| LIBYAN-BACKED TERROR | In the 1990s, Libya began to distance itself from foreign terrorist groups and to crack down on terrorists in Libya. In the early 2000s, the country helped U.S. officials hunt down al-Qaeda terrorists. In 2003 Muammar Qadhafi announced that Libya would dismantle its weapons of mass destruction.

| BRITAIN AND NORTHERN IRELAND | In the 1990s, the PIRA began to use peaceful methods to pursue its political goals. The PIRA and other terrorist groups signed the Good Friday Agreement in 1998. The treaty called for Irish terrorist groups to disarm and gave people in Northern Ireland more control of their own political affairs.

| SRI LANKA AND THE LTTE | The conflict between the LTTE and government fighters in Sri Lanka continued throughout the 1990s. But the LTTE and the government agreed to a cease-fire in late 2001 and began peace talks in 2002. Under terms of the peace agreement, the Tamils were given limited self-rule.

| TURKEY AND THE KURDS | Since Abdullah Ocalan's capture, the PKK has changed its approach. The group reorganized itself as a political party, called the Congress for Freedom and Democracy in Kurdistan. The party says it will fight for Kurdish rights using peaceful political means. ∎

*Please note that the information contained in this book was current at the time of publication. To find sources for late-breaking news, please consult the websites listed on page 69.

TIMELINE

Islamic	Libya
Israel and Palestine	Britain and Northern Ireland
Sri Lanka and the LTTE	Turkey and the Kurds

1948 Israel becomes an independent nation. War breaks out between Israel and neighboring Arab states.

1964 The Palestinian Liberation Organization is founded.

1967 Israel seizes Palestinian territory (including the present-day occupied territories) in the Six-Day War.

1968 Israel's Sayeret Mat'kal fighters attack the Beirut International Airport in retaliation for terrorist attacks on Israeli targets. Ahmed Jibril founds the Popular Front for the Liberation of Palestine General Command.

1969 Palestinians found the Democratic Front for the Liberation of Palestine.

1970 Ahmed Jibril carries out bombings against Swiss and Austrian airliners bound for Israel. Muammar Qadhafi takes over Libya's government. The Provisional Irish Republican Army is founded.

1971 Palestinian fighters found Black September.

1972 Black September terrorists kill eleven Israeli athletes at the Olympic Games in Munich, Germany.

1973 Israel carries out Operation Spring of Youth in retaliation for the Munich Olympic massacre. Palestinian fighters assassinate a U.S. diplomat in Khartoum, Sudan. Abu Jihad becomes military commander of the PLO.

1976 Tamil fighters found the Liberation Tigers of Tamil Eelam in Sri Lanka.

1978 Abdullah Ocalan creates the Kurdistan Workers Party.

1979 Islamic extremists seize the U.S. Embassy in Tehran, Iran, taking a group of Americans hostage.

1983 Islamic terrorists bomb the U.S. Embassy in Beirut, Lebanon. A suicide bomber drives a truck into a U.S. Marines barracks in Beirut, killing 241 marines.

1985 Abu Jihad tries to attack Israel's Defense Ministry buildings in Tel Aviv.

1986 Libya fires surface-to-air missiles at U.S. Navy jets near the Libyan coast. Libyan agents bomb La Belle Discotheque in West Berlin, Germany. The United States carries out Operation El Dorado Canyon, attacking Libyan targets in retaliation for La Belle Discotheque bombing.

1987 The intifada begins in the occupied territories. Army Commando Regiment units ambush Liberation Tigers of Tamil Eelam forces in Sri Lanka. British forces carry out Operation Judy to thwart a PIRA attack on an RUC station in Northern Ireland.

1988 Palestinian terrorists blow up Pan Am Flight 103 over Lockerbie, Scotland. A PLO terrorist squad tries to attack an Israeli nuclear plant. Israeli forces assassinate PLO leader Abu Jihad. Israeli forces carry out Operation Blue and Brown, attacking Ahmed Jibril's headquarters in Lebanon. British agents carry out Operation Flavius, trying to stop a suspected PIRA attack on a British fortress in Gibraltar.

1989 Islamic terrorists found al-Qaeda, a worldwide Islamic terrorist organization.

1996 The Taliban seizes power in Afghanistan.

1998 The Syrian government closes down PKK facilities and expels Abdullah Ocalan from Syria.

1999 Turkish forces capture Abdullah Ocalan in Kenya.

2001 Planes crash in New York City; Washington, D.C.; and Pennsylvania, killing approximately three thousand people in the September 11 terrorist attacks organized by al-Quada. U.S., British, and Afghan forces overthrow the Taliban in Afghanistan.

2002 U.S. and other coalition forces carry out Operation Anaconda, attacking al-Qaeda fighters hiding in Afghanistan. U.S. and Pakistani forces capture Ramzi Binalshibh, a leader in the September 11, 2001, attacks.

SELECTED BIBLIOGRAPHY

Bolger, Daniel. *Americans at War.* Novato, CA: Presidio Press, 1988.

Conboy, Ken. *Elite Forces of India and Pakistan.* London: Osprey, 1992.

Cooley, John, K. *Payback: America's Long War in the Middle East.* McLean, VA: Brassey's, 1991.

———. *Unholy Wars: Afghanistan, America, and International Terrorism.* London: Pluto Press, 2000.

Coulson, Danny O., and Elaine Shannon. *No Heroes: Inside the FBI's Secret Counter-Terror Force.* New York: Pocket Books, 1999.

Davies, Barry. *SAS Shadow Warriors of the 21st Century.* Miami: Lewis International, Inc., 2002.

Dobson, Christopher, and Ronald Payne. *Counterattack: The West's Battle against the Terrorists.* New York: Facts on File, 1982.

Emerson, Steven. *Secret Warriors: Inside the Covert Military Operations of the Reagan Era.* New York: Putnam, 1988.

Geraghty, Tony. *Who Dares Wins: The Special Air Service—1950 to the Gulf War.* London: Bantam Books, 1992.

Haney, Eric. *Inside Delta Force: The Story of America's Elite Counterterrorist Unit.* New York: Delacorte Press, 2002.

Harnden, Toby. *Bandit Country: The IRA and South Armagh.* Edinburgh: Hodder and Sloughton, 1999.

Katz, Samuel, M. *The Elite.* New York: Pocket Books, 1992.

———. *The Night Raiders: Israel Naval Commandos at War.* New York: Pocket Books, 1997.

Moore, Robin. *The Hunt for Bin Laden: Task Force Dagger.* New York: Random House, 2003.

Urban, Mark. *Big Boys' Rules: The Secret Struggle against the IRA.* London: Faber and Faber, 1992.

Zonder, Moshe. *Sayeret Mat'kal.* Tel Aviv: Keter Publishing House Ltd., 2000.

FURTHER READING AND WEBSITES

Books

Black, Eric. *Northern Ireland: Troubled Land.* Minneapolis: Lerner Publications Company, 1998.

Bodnarchuk, Kari. *Kurdistan: Region under Siege.* Minneapolis: Lerner Publications Company, 2000.

Currie, Stephen. *Terrorists and Terrorist Groups.* San Diego: Lucent Books, 2002.

Goldstein, Margaret J. *Israel in Pictures.* Minneapolis: Lerner Publications Company, 2004.

Headlam, George. *Yasser Arafat.* Minneapolis: Lerner Publications Company, 2004.

Katz, Sam. *Against All Odds: Counterterrorist Hostage Rescues.* Minneapolis: Lerner Publications Company, 2005.

———. *At Any Cost: National Liberation Terrorism.* Minneapolis: Lerner Publications Company, 2004.

———. *Jerusalem or Death: Palestinian Terrorism.* Minneapolis: Lerner Publications Company, 2004.

———. *Jihad: Islamic Fundamentalist Terrorism.* Minneapolis: Lerner Publications Company, 2004.

———. *Raging Within: Ideological Terrorism.* Minneapolis: Lerner Publications Company, 2004.

———. *Targeting Terror: Counterterrorist Raids.* Minneapolis: Lerner Publications Company, 2005.

———. *U.S. Counterstrike: American Counterterrorism.* Minneapolis: Lerner Publications Company, 2005.

Kushner, Harvey W. *Encyclopedia of Terrorism.* Newbury Park, CA: Sage Publications, 2003.

Woolf, Alex. *Osama bin Laden.* Minneapolis: Lerner Publications Company, 2004.

Zwier, Lawrence J. *Sri Lanka: War-Torn Island.* Minneapolis: Lerner Publications Company, 1998.

Websites

BBC News:World Edition
<http://news.bbc.co.uk>
This website offers extensive international coverage and analysis of news and events.

CNN.com
<http://www.cnn.com>
This site provides the lastest news on world conflicts and terrorism.

International Policy Institute for Counter-Terrorism
<http://www.ict.org.il>
This site features up-to-date news and commentary on international terrorism, as well a sections on terrorist organizations and the Arab-Israeli conflict.

Terrorism Questions and Answers
<http://terrorismanswers.com>
This site is operated by the Council on Foreign Relations and the Markle Foundation. It provides information on terrorism and terrorist groups in a question-and-answer format.

The Terrorism Research Center
<http://www.terrorism.com>
In addition to historic information on terrorist groups, this site also provides antiterrorist information and links to other useful sites.

Terrorist Group Profiles
<http://library.nps.navy.mil/home/tgp/tgp2.htm>
This website features profiles of terrorist groups, chronologies of terrorist incidents, and a link to the U.S. State Department.

U.S. Department of State Counterterrorism Office
<http://www.state.gov/s/ct>
The U.S. government maintains this site offering information on historic and active terrorist groups.

INDEX

ABOUT THE AUTHOR

Samuel M. Katz is an expert in the fields of international terrorism and counterterrorism, military special operations, and law enforcement. He has written more than twenty books and dozens of articles on these subjects. He is the editor in chief of *Special Operations Report* (www.specialoperationsreport.com). He has also created documentary films and lectured to law-enforcement and counterterrorist agencies around the world. The Terrorist Dossiers series is his first foray into the field of nonfiction for young people.

PHOTO ACKNOWLEDGMENTS

The images in this book are used with the permission of: © Francoise de Mulder/CORBIS, p. 10; © Bettmann/CORBIS, pp. 11, 17; The State of Israel National Photo Collection, pp. 12, 36; © Hulton|Archive by Getty Images, p. 14; © AFP/Getty Images, pp. 15, 51, 60; © Ullstein/Rondholz, p. 19; © Bernard Bisson/CORBIS SYMA, p. 20; © Dinodia Picture Agency, p. 22; AP/Wide World Photos, pp. 24 (left), 30, 41 (bottom), 44, 52; Independent Picture Service, p. 24 (inset); Imperial War Museum, London, p. 28; © Bill Pierce/Time Life Pictures/Getty Images, p. 29; © Art Directors/J. Wakelin, p. 31; © Art Directors/J. Highet, p. 34; Topham Picturepoint, p. 35; © David Rubinger/Time Life Pictures/Getty Images, p. 38; © Reza/Webistan/CORBIS, p. 41 (top); Alpert Nathan/State of Israel National Photo Collection, p. 42; © M. Attar/CORBIS SYGMA, p. 49; © Hussein Abou Kha/Attar Maher/ CORBIS SYGMA, p. 50; © Reuters/CORBIS, pp. 54, 56 (top); © Samuel M. Katz, p. 56 (bottom); © Scott Nelson/Getty Images, p. 57; © Lynsey Addario/CORBIS, p. 59; © Getty Images, p. 61; Defense Visual Information Center, p. 62; © Zahid Hussein/Reuters/Landov, p. 64. Cover: © Zahid Hussein/Reuters/Landov